AF334323

❦ *Times of Challenge* ❧

TIMES OF CHALLENGE

Thoughts About Life
as expressed by
Anne Morrow Lindbergh
Albert Schweitzer
Dag Hammarskjöld
Rose Kennedy
and many more

NORCROSS

Grateful acknowledgment is made to the following for permission to reprint previously published material:

Doubleday & Company, Inc.: excerpt from the Introduction by Anne Birstein and Alfred Kazin from *The Works of Anne Frank*. Copyright © 1959 by Otto H. Frank; excerpt from *The Open Door* by Helen Keller. Bernard Geis Associates, Inc.: excerpt from *Mr. Citizen* by Harry S. Truman. Copyright © 1953, 1957, 1958, 1959, 1960 by Harry Truman. Harper & Row, Publishers, Inc.: and Nannine Joseph for excerpts from *You Learn by Living* by Eleanor Roosevelt. Copyright © 1960 by Eleanor Roosevelt; excerpt from *The Nobel Lecture on Literature* by Aleksandr I. Solzhenitsyn, translated by Thomas P. Whitney. Copyright © 1972 by The Nobel Foundation, English copyright © 1972 by Thomas P. Whitney; excerpt from *Profiles in Courage* by John Fitzgerald Kennedy. Copyright © 1956 by John Fitzgerald Kennedy. Holt, Rinehart and Winston, Inc.: and George Allen and Unwin Ltd. for excerpt from *Out of My Life and Thought* by Albert Schweitzer, translated by C. T. Campion. Houghton Mifflin Company: excerpt from *Lou Gehrig: The Iron Horse of Baseball* by Richard G. Hubler. Copyright © 1941 and 1968 by Richard G. Hubler. Alfred A. Knopf, Inc.: and Faber and Faber Ltd., for excerpt from *Markings* by Dag Hammarskjöld, translated by Leif Sjoberg and W. H. Auden. Copyright © 1964 by Alfred A. Knopf, Inc. and Faber and Faber Ltd.; and Jonathan Cape Limited for excerpt from *My Young Years* by Arthur Rubinstein. Copyright © 1973 by Amela Rubinstein, Eva Rubinstein Coffin, Alina Anna Rubinstein, and John Arthur Rubinstein. Little, Brown and Company: and Paul R. Reynolds, Inc., 12 East 41st Street, New York, N.Y. 10017, for excerpt from *It's Good to Be Alive* by Roy Campanella. Copyright © 1959 by Roy Campanella. David McKay Company, Inc.: excerpt from *Will Rogers* by Donald Day. Copyright © 1962 by Donald Day. G. P. Putnam's Sons: and The Hamlyn Group Ltd. for excerpt from *Great Destiny* by Winston S. Churchill, Edited by F. W. Heath. Copyright © 1962, 1965 by Odran's Press Ltd., London and A. M. Heath & Co. Ltd. for excerpt from *Rose: A Biography of Rose Fitzgerald Kennedy* by Gail Cameron. Copyright © 1971 by Gail Cameron. Random House, Inc.: excerpts from *The Essential Gandhi* by Louis Fischer. Copyright © 1962 by Louis Fischer; excerpt from *Count Your Blessings* by Israel Chodos. Copyright © 1955 by Israel Chodos; excerpt from *As I Live and Breathe* by Malcolm Boyd. Copyright © 1965, 1968, 1969 by Malcolm Boyd; and Justice Douglas and The Lantz Office Inc. for excerpt from *Go East Young Man: The Early Years* by William O. Douglas. Copyright © 1974 by William O. Douglas. The Viking Press, Inc.: excerpt from *My Lord What a Morning* by Marian Anderson. Copyright © 1956 by Marian Anderson.

Creative Director: Eleanor Ehrhardt

Associate: Sue Tarsky

Design Assistant: Charlotte Staub

Photographs: Frederick C. Bruns; D. M. Goddard;

Charles R. Luchsinger; George Popper.

☞ Keep your fears to yourself, but share your courage with others.

Robert Louis Stevenson

The encouraging thing is that every time you meet a situation, though you may think at the time it is an impossibility and you go through the tortures of the damned, once you have met it and lived through it you find that forever after you are freer than you ever were before. If you can live through that you can live through anything. You gain strength, courage, and confidence by every experience in which you really stop to look fear in the face.

You are able to say to yourself, "I lived through this horror. I can take the next thing that comes along."

Eleanor Roosevelt

I
COUNT
ONLY
SUNNY HOURS

There is a time in every man's education when he arrives at the conviction that envy is ignorance; that imitation is suicide; that he must take himself for better for worse as his portion; that though the wide universe is full of good, no kernel of nourishing corn can come to him but through his toil bestowed on that plot of ground which is given to him to till. The power which resides in him is new in nature, and none but he knows what that is which he can do, nor does he know until he has tried. Not for nothing one face, one character, one fact, makes much impression on him, and another none. This sculpture in the memory is not without pre-established harmony. The eye was placed where one ray should fall, that it might testify of that particular ray. We but half express ourselves, and are ashamed of that divine idea which each of us represents. It may be safely trusted as proportionate and of good issues, so it be faithfully imparted, but God will not have his work made manifest by cowards. A man is relieved and gay when he has put his heart into his work and done his best; but what he has said or done otherwise shall give him no peace. It is a deliverance which does not deliver. In the attempt his genius deserts him; no muse befriends; no invention, no hope.

Ralph Waldo Emerson

As courage and intelligence are the two qualities best worth a good man's cultivation, so it is the first part of intelligence to recognize our precarious estate in life, and the first part of courage to be not at all abashed before the fact. A frank and somewhat headlong carriage, not looking too anxiously before, not dallying in maudlin regret over the past, stamps the man who is well armoured for this world.

Robert Louis Stevenson

There is no principle worth the name if it is not wholly good. I swear by non-violence because I know that it alone conduces to the highest good of mankind, not merely in the next world, but in this also. I object to violence because, when it appears to do good, the good is only temporary, the evil it does is permanent. . . .

Mahatma Gandhi

I do not grudge our loyal, brave people, who were ready to do their duty no matter what the cost, who never flinched under the strain of last week—I do not grudge them the natural, spontaneous outburst of joy and relief when they learned that the hard ordeal would no longer be required of them at the moment; but they should know the truth. They should know that there has been gross neglect and deficiency in our defences; they should know that we have sustained a defeat without a war, the consequences of which will travel far with us along our road; they should know that we have passed an awful milestone in our history, when the whole equilibrium of Europe has been deranged, and that the terrible words have for the time being been pronounced against the Western democracies: "Thou art weighed in the balance and found wanting." And do not suppose that this is the end. This is only the beginning of the reckoning. This is only the first sip, the first foretaste of a bitter cup which will be proferred to us year by year unless, by a supreme recovery of moral health and martial vigour, we arise again and take our stand for freedom as in the olden time.

Winston S. Churchill

9

It should be the object of all to avoid controversy, to allay passions, give full scope to reason and every kindly feeling. By doing this and encouraging our citizens to engage in the duties of life with all their heart and mind, with a determination not to be turned aside by thoughts of the past and fears of the future, our country will not only be restored in material prosperity, but will be advanced in science, in virtue and in religion.

Robert E. Lee

I *am* very lucky, but I have a little theory about this. I have noticed through experience and through my own observations that providence, Nature, God, or what I would call the Power of Creation seems to favor human beings who accept and love life unconditionally. And I am certainly one who does, with all my heart. So I have discovered as a result of what I can only call miracles that whenever my inner self desires something subconsciously, life will somehow grant it to me.

Arthur Rubinstein

We have been given a miraculous
faculty: to be able to communicate de-
spite differences in languages, customs,
and social structures the life-experience
of one whole nation to another whole
nation—to communicate a difficult na-
tional experience many decades long
which the second nation has never ex-
perienced at all. And in the most favor-
able case this may save a whole nation
from a path which is unnecessary, or mis-
taken, or even fatal. And in this way the
twistings and windings of human history
are lessened.

Simple is the ordinary courageous
human being's act of not participating in
the lie, of not supporting false actions!
What his stand says is: "So be it that *this*
takes place in the world, that it even
reigns in the world—but let it not be with
my complicity."

Aleksandr J. Solzhenitsyn

⇜§ I believe with a perfect faith that we who have outdistanced all previous generations in the discovery of the great truths of our physical world, can yet find the answer to some of the unsolved riddles of the universe which will ultimately spell out the happiness of humanity, as well. For man is happily obsessed with a spiritual claustrophobia that makes him push the walls of the world apart. Everest *must* be climbed and Annapurna *must* be conquered. The deepest caves of the earth and the world beneath the sea *must* be explored. Man scales the altitudes and plumbs the depths and bestrides the plateaus of his world like a colossus. Yet every new conquest brings a newer quest.

And the end is nowhere in sight.

Israel Chodos ßↄ

∾ There are many persons ready to do what is right because in their hearts they know it is right. But they hesitate, waiting for the other fellow to make the first move—and he, in turn, waits for you. The minute a person whose word means a great deal dares to take the open-hearted and courageous way, many others follow.

Marian Anderson

In spite of the great importance we attach to the triumphs of knowledge and achievement, it is nevertheless obvious that only a humanity which is striving after ethical ends can in full measure share in the blessings brought by material progress and become master of the dangers which accompany it.

Albert Schweitzer

I've learned that nobody who is allowed the luxury of being alive has a right to get too worked up over trouble. Why? Because trouble is what makes a man put out and bring off a better job than he'd do without it. After all, we all have our built-in troubles and I think that maybe God put them in our path to make us toe the mark a little sharper.

Thinking on trouble, I know that when it strikes, if you can manage to meet it head on, smile at it and roll up your sleeves to beat it, God takes a hand. He gives you an inner strength. It don't show like muscles, maybe, but it's stronger and more lasting than muscles. I found that to be so. I don't really have much any more in the way of muscles, but I got something else that's better and stronger. God.

Roy Campanella

How lovely to think that no one need wait a moment, we can start now, start slowly changing the world! How lovely that everyone, great and small, can make their contribution toward introducing justice straight away! Just as with so many things, most people seek justice in quite another quarter, they grumble because they receive so little of it themselves. Open your eyes, first make sure that you are always fair yourself! Give of yourself, give as much as you can! And you can always give something, even if it is only kindness! If everyone were to do this and not be as mean with a kindly word, then there would be much more justice and love in the world. Give and you shall receive, much more than you would have ever thought possible. Give, give again and again, don't lose courage, keep it up and go on giving! No one has ever become poor from giving! If you do this, then in a few generations no one will need to pity the beggar children any more, because they will not exist!

There is plenty of room for everyone in the world, enough money, riches, and beauty for all to share! God has made enough for everyone! Let us all begin then by sharing it fairly.

Anne Frank

⁊ I suppose that most of us, if we were asked to name the most profound issues at stake in the world today, would say the issues of freedom and democracy. We would say that the Western world, for all its errors and shortcomings, has tried for centuries to evolve a society in which the individual has enough legal, social and political elbow room to be not the puppet of the community, but his own autonomous self.

And we would say that the enemies of freedom, whatever the magnificent ends they propose—the brotherhood of man, the kingdom of saints, "from each according to his ability, to each according to his needs"—miss just this essential point: that man is greater than the social purposes to which he can be put. He must not be kicked about even with the most high-minded objectives. He is not a means or an instrument. He is an end in himself.

This, I take it, is the essence of what we mean by democracy—not so much voting systems or parliamentary systems or economic or legal systems (though they all enter in), as an irrevocable and final dedication to the dignity of man.

Adlai Stevenson ॐ

Most of my own ideas on how the world runs I obtained very early in life from the Bible, the King James version of the Old and the New Testaments. The Bible is, among other things, one of the greatest documents of history. Every trouble that humanity is heir to is set out in the Bible. And the remedy is there, too, if you know where to find it. I read the Bible at least a dozen times, and maybe more, before I was fifteen years old. The Bible must be read over and over again to get the full meaning out of it. The same is true of the Constitution of the United States.

And the moral code that is in the Old and New Testaments is needed by all mankind. If civilization is to continue, the majority of the people of the world must have a moral code by which to live, and by which to act. The moral code set forth in the Bible is unequalled. Of course, these youngsters in whom I am so vitally interested will be brought up on a moral code, I hope, based on the great code of the Old and New Testaments.

Harry S Truman

I am an irrepressible optimist, because I believe in myself. That sounds very arrogant, doesn't it? But I say it from the depths of my humility. . . . I am an optimist because I expect many things from myself. I have not got them, I know, as I am not yet a perfect being. . . . I want to attain that perfection by service.

Mahatma Gandhi

That state of life is most happy where superfluities are not required and necessities are not wanting.

Plutarch

❦ **H**uman felicity is produced not so much by great pieces of good fortune that seldom happen, as by little advantages that occur every day.

Benjamin Franklin ❧

If conquests useful to humanity touch your heart, if you stand amazed before the surprising effects of electric telegraphy, the daguerrotype, anesthesia and so many other admirable discoveries: if you are jealous of the part your country can claim in the further flowering of these wonders—take an interest, I urge upon you, in those holy dwellings to which the expressive name of laboratories is given. Ask that they be multiplied and adorned. They are the temples of the future, of wealth and well-being. It is there that humanity grows bigger, strengthens and betters itself. It learns there to read in the works of nature, works of progress and universal harmony, whereas its own works are too often those of barbarity, fanaticism and destruction.

Louis Pasteur

I am among those who think that science has great beauty. A scientist in his laboratory is not only a technician: he is also a child placed before natural phenomena which impress him like a fairy tale. We should not allow it to be believed that all scientific progress can be reduced to mechanisms, machines, gearings, even though such machinery also has its own beauty.

Neither do I believe that the spirit of adventure runs any risk of disappearing in our world. If I see anything vital around me, it is precisely that spirit of adventure, which seems indestructible and is akin to curiosity. . . .

Marie Curie

Duty to France, duty to the Empire, forbid hesitation, false prudence, cowardly circumspection. In the enormous upheaval, all that has any meaning or value are men who can think, will, and act according to the terrible rhythm of events. The others will be swept away.

Charles De Gaulle

A man who has never been in danger cannot answer for his courage.

La Rochefoucauld

Do not be too timid and squeamish about your actions. All life is an experiment. The more experiments you make the better. What if they are a little coarse, and you may get your coat soiled or torn? What if you do fail, and get fairly rolled in the dirt once or twice? Up again, you shall never be so afraid of a tumble.

Ralph Waldo Emerson

The secret of Happiness is Freedom, and the secret of Freedom, Courage.

Thucydides

I'd rather give my life than be afraid to give it.

Lyndon Baines Johnson

I just made up my mind that I wasn't going to be vanquished by anything. If I collapsed, then it would have a very bad effect on the other members of the family, naturally. . . . And I think I owe them a certain calmness and encouragement, and that's what I try to do.

Rose Fitzgerald Kennedy

One hour of life, crowded to the full with glorious action, and filled with noble risks, is worth whole years of those mean observances of petty decorum, in which men steal through existence, like sluggish waters through a marsh, without either honor or observation.

Sir Walter Scott

∾ I desire so to conduct the affairs of this administration that if at the end, when I have come to lay down the reins of power, I have lost every other friend on earth, I shall at least have one friend left, and that friend shall be down inside me.

Abraham Lincoln ∾

∾ He who receives an idea from me, receives instruction himself without lessening mine; as he who lights his taper at mine, receives light without darkening me.

Thomas Jefferson ∾

In such a time, in the face of such a tide, I must affirm my belief in the individual. I affirm my trust in the individual human heart. I place my emphasis upon the single human mind. No, more, I say that the lowest mind is the mass mind. When men bind themselves together their minds lose clarity, as the brooks do, as the river does, and they overflow into like destruction. I say the coldest, hardest, most inhuman heart is the mass heart, which has lost all sense of individual need, so that it views life and death with callous equal indifference. The most deadened soul is the mass soul, which has no generosities, no impulse of kindness or understanding, no spiritual denominator. That which is common to all is nearest the beast.

Therefore, if I have anything to say, it is to beg men and women never to give themselves up entirely to any cause or creed or mass or race or belief. What each of us has to give of most worth is that which is most peculiarly individual in us. That peculiar individuality is as well our most delicate means of

receiving from others what is most valuable and ex-
quisite in life. To lose it is to lose at once our means
of receiving the best from others and giving the best
of ourselves. To keep it is to keep ourselves clear
and untrammeled by confusions; it is to maintain
in ourselves a center of tranquillity in a stormy and
disheveled world. John Doe is forever himself also,
not only one among millions. His life is of value in so
far as he most realizes himself. Long ago someone
said, "And what shall it profit a man if he lose his
own soul?" It is a question to ask again today.

Pearl S. Buck 🙐

When evil men plot, good men must plan.
When evil men burn and bomb, good men must build
and bind. When evil men shout ugly words of hatred,
good men must commit themselves to the glories of
love. When evil men would seek to perpetuate an
unjust status quo, good men must seek to bring into
being a real order of justice.

Martin Luther King, Jr. 🙐

es They say I've had a bad break. But when the office force and the ground-keepers and even the Giants from across the river whom we'd give our right arm to beat in the World Series—when they remember you, that's something. And when you even have a mother-in-law who takes sides against her own daughter, that's something.

And when you have a wonderful father and mother who worked hard to give you an education, that's something. And when you have a wonderful wife who has shown more courage than I ever hope to have, that's really great.

And when you have spent six years with a great little manager like Miller Huggins and the next nine with the finest and smartest manager in baseball today, Joe McCarthy—and when you have the privilege of rooming, eating, playing cards, and knowing one of the greatest fellows that ever lived, Bill Dickey—

I may have been given a bad break but I've an awful lot to live for. With all this, I consider myself the luckiest man on the face of the earth.

Lou Gehrig

Only life can satisfy the demands of life. And this hunger of mine can be satisfied for the simple reason that the nature of life is such that I can realize my individuality by becoming a bridge for others, a stone in the temple of righteousness.

Don't be afraid of yourself, live your individuality to the full—but for the good of others. Don't copy others in order to buy fellowship, or make convention your law instead of living the righteousness.

To become free and responsible. For this alone was man created, and he who fails to take the Way which could have been his shall be lost eternally.

Dag Hammarskjöld

Death dident scare her. It was only an episode in her life. If you live right, death is a Joke to you as far as fear is concerned. I have today witnessed a Funeral that for real sorrow and real affection I don't think will ever be surpassed anywhere. They came on foot, in Buggies, Horseback, Wagons, Cars and Train, and there wasent a Soul that come that she hadent helped or favored at one time or another. Some uninformed Newspapers printed: "Mrs. C. L. Lane, sister of the famous Comedian, Will Rogers." It's the other way around. I am the brother of Mrs. C. L. Lane, "The Friend of Humanity." And all the honors that I could ever in my wildest dreams hope to reach would never equal the honor paid on a little Western Prairie hilltop, among her people, to Maude Lane. *If they will love me like that at the finish, my life will not have been in vain.*

Will Rogers

Our greatest happiness . . . does not depend on the condition of life in which chance has placed us, but is always the result of a good conscience, good health, occupation, and freedom in all just pursuits.

Thomas Jefferson

We vote as many, but we pray as one. With a united people, with faith in democracy, with common concern for others less fortunate around the globe, we shall move forward with God's guidance toward the time when His children shall grow in freedom and dignity in a world at peace.

Adlai Stevenson

What I must do is all that concerns me, not what the people think. This rule, equally arduous in actual and in intellectual life, may serve for the whole distinction between greatness and meanness. It is the harder because you will always find those who think they know what is your duty better than you know it. It is easy in the world to live after the world's opinion; it is easy in solitude to live after our own; but the great man is he who in the midst of the crowd keeps with perfect sweetness the independence of solitude.

Ralph Waldo Emerson

Relationship, I have learned, has a nerve of commitment to it. "For better for worse, for richer for poorer, in sickness and in health, to love and to cherish": these are words not alone for the marriage of a man and a woman. These words are a vow for all people in relationship—between friends, in a job, between neighbors, on a campus, in the city, everywhere.

Relationship with anyone is a specific symbol of one's basic, pervasive responsibility for the universe outside oneself. Any relationship therefore signifies one's membership in the human race.

Malcolm Boyd

Life and death, profit and loss, failure and success, poverty and wealth, value and worthlessness, praise and blame, hunger and thirst, cold and heat—these are natural changes in the order of things. They alternate with one another like day and night. No one knows where one ends and the other begins. Therefore, they should not disturb our peace or enter our souls. Live so that you are at ease, in harmony with the world, and full of joy. Day and night, share the springtime with all things, thus creating the seasons in your own heart. This is called achieving full harmony.

Confucius

&ersand; The only thing we have to fear is fear itself—nameless, unreasoning, unjustified terror which paralyzes needed efforts to convert retreat into advance.

Franklin Delano Roosevelt

By the time FDR made this speech, I had learned from personal experiences that he spoke the truth.

Fear is man's worst enemy, and many of his fears come from imponderables that the victim often does not even suspect. The person who cannot without great apprehension enter an elevator or an airplane or other locked vehicle may be a casualty of a severe birth trauma. Fear of water, fear of lightning, fear of the darkness, fear of animals, fear of open spaces can also be real and forbidding.

I suppose few people started life with more fears than I—and few reached the thirties with less. The best way of riddance is talking with a knowledgeable person. I had few of those opportunities as I grew up, since I had no adult confidant. Most of my fears were resolved by confrontation and rationalization—the hardest but certainly the most enduring way.

William O. Douglas

Anyone who, out of goodness of his heart, speaks a helpful word, gives a cheering smile, or smooths over a rough place in another's path knows that the delight he feels is so intimate a part of himself that he lives by it. The joy of surmounting obstacles which once seemed unremovable, and pushing the frontier of accomplishment further— what joy is there like unto it? If those who seek happiness would only stop one little minute and think, they would see that the delights they really experience are as countless as the grasses at their feet or the dewdrops sparkling upon the morning flowers.

Helen Keller

A slender acquaintance with the world must convince every man that actions, not words, are the true criterion of the attachment of friends; and that the most liberal professions of good-will are very far from being the surest marks of it.

There exists in the economy and course of nature an indissoluble union between virtue and happiness, between duty and advantage, between the genuine maxims of an honest and magnanimous policy and the solid rewards of public prosperity and felicity.

George Washington

⇛ The courage of life is often a less dramatic spectacle than the courage of a final moment; but it is no less than a magnificent mixture of triumph and tragedy. A man does what he must—in spite of personal consequences, in spite of obstacles and dangers and pressures—and that is the basis of all human morality.

John F. Kennedy ∽

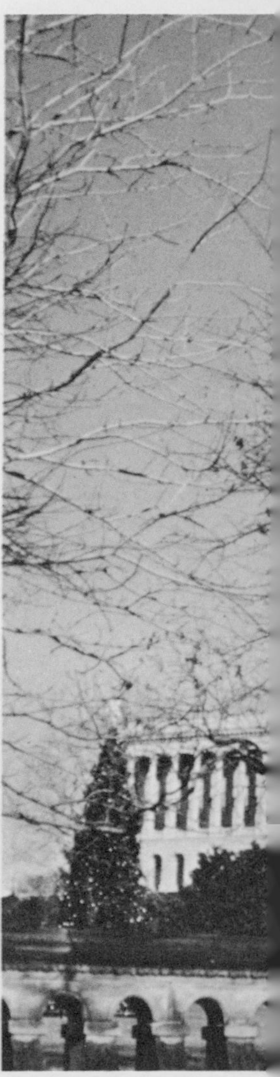

&8 It is a brave thing to have courage
to be an individual; it is also, perhaps, a
lonely thing. But it is better than not being
an individual, which is to be nobody at all.

Eleanor Roosevelt &8